Ham with Jam

Illustrated by Karen Bell

High-Frequency Words

with   a

Editorial Offices: Glenview, Illinois • Parsippany, New Jersey • New York, New York
Sales Offices: Parsippany, New Jersey • Duluth, Georgia • Glenview, Illinois
Coppell, Texas • Ontario, California

Diz and Rex set up a box.

Diz got a bun and jam.

Rex got a bun and ham.

Get a bun with jam!

Get jam on a bun!

Get a bun with ham!

Get ham on a bun!

Jan and Nat had a
bun with jam. Yum!

Ted and Ben had
ham on a bun. Yum!

Diz and Rex had

ham with jam. Yum?

Ham with Jam

Illustrated by Karen Bell

High-Frequency Words
with   a

Scott
Foresman

Editorial Offices: Glenview, Illinois • Parsippany, New Jersey • New York, New York
Sales Offices: Parsippany, New Jersey • Duluth, Georgia • Glenview, Illinois
Coppell, Texas • Ontario, California

Diz and Rex set up a box.

Diz got a bun and jam.

Rex got a bun and ham.

Get a bun with jam!

Get jam on a bun!

Get a bun with ham!

Get ham on a bun!

Jan and Nat had a
bun with jam. Yum!

Ted and Ben had
ham on a bun. Yum!

Diz and Rex had

ham with jam. Yum?

Ham with Jam

Illustrated by Karen Bell

High-Frequency Words
with   a

Scott Foresman

Editorial Offices: Glenview, Illinois • Parsippany, New Jersey • New York, New York
Sales Offices: Parsippany, New Jersey • Duluth, Georgia • Glenview, Illinois
Coppell, Texas • Ontario, California

Diz and Rex set up a box.

Diz got a bun and jam.

Rex got a bun and ham.

Get a bun with jam!

Get jam on a bun!

Get a bun with ham!

Get ham on a bun!

Jan and Nat had a
bun with jam. Yum!

Ted and Ben had
ham on a bun. Yum!

Diz and Rex had

ham with jam. Yum?

Ham with Jam

Illustrated by Karen Bell

High-Frequency Words

with   a

Editorial Offices: Glenview, Illinois • Parsippany, New Jersey • New York, New York
Sales Offices: Parsippany, New Jersey • Duluth, Georgia • Glenview, Illinois
Coppell, Texas • Ontario, California

Diz and Rex set up a box.

Diz got a bun and jam.

Rex got a bun and ham.

Get a bun with jam!

Get jam on a bun!

Get a bun with ham!

Get ham on a bun!

Jan and Nat had a
bun with jam. Yum!

6

Ted and Ben had
ham on a bun. Yum!

Diz and Rex had
ham with jam. Yum?

Ham with Jam

Illustrated by Karen Bell

High-Frequency Words	
with	a

Editorial Offices: Glenview, Illinois • Parsippany, New Jersey • New York, New York
Sales Offices: Parsippany, New Jersey • Duluth, Georgia • Glenview, Illinois
Coppell, Texas • Ontario, California

Diz and Rex set up a box.

Diz got a bun and jam.

Rex got a bun and ham.

Get a bun with jam!

Get jam on a bun!

Get a bun with ham!

Get ham on a bun!

Jan and Nat had a
bun with jam. Yum!

Ted and Ben had

ham on a bun. Yum!

Diz and Rex had

ham with jam. Yum?

Ham with Jam

Illustrated by Karen Bell

High-Frequency Words

with   a

Scott
Foresman

Editorial Offices: Glenview, Illinois • Parsippany, New Jersey • New York, New York
Sales Offices: Parsippany, New Jersey • Duluth, Georgia • Glenview, Illinois
Coppell, Texas • Ontario, California

Diz and Rex set up a box.

Diz got a bun and jam.

Rex got a bun and ham.

Get a bun with jam!

Get jam on a bun!

Get a bun with ham!

Get ham on a bun!

Jan and Nat had a
bun with jam. Yum!

6

Ted and Ben had
ham on a bun. Yum!

Diz and Rex had
ham with jam. Yum?